D.A.T.
DEFENSIVE ARTS TRAINING

D.A.T.
DEFENSIVE ARTS TRAINING

Manual and Study Guide Vol. 1

Written & Illustrations by
Master Dwayne A. Thomas
Founder & Chief Instructor

To order additional copies of this book, contact:
Xlibris Corporation
1-888-795-4274
www.Xlibris.com
Orders@Xlibris.com
54907

DEDICATION

I dedicate this book respectfully to all my dear students, friends and entire family, who have stood by me and supported me through out my life journey in training. To all my instructors for without whom this would not have been possible. Remember to believe in your self and in your dreams so that one day it will become your reality.

Master Dwayne A. Thomas
Founder and Instructor of D.A.T.
10th Degree Black Belt

Author's Introduction

I am the founder and Chief Instructor of Defensive Arts Training System which is an eclectic style. I have been active within the martial art for over 25 years. This style of martial arts combines the many art forms and disciplines, which I have been trained in throughout my years of study. These styles range from Traditional hard Japanese to the soft and flowing Chinese Kung Fu and Tai Chi. I began studying the arts at about the tender age of 13 in the mean streets of New York City in the South Bronx. Some of my Masters were also former U.S. military men who have served in many wars and train in hand-to-hand combat.

I received my first black belt rank in the arts in 1975. In the early 80's I began teaching and instructing others in the art of self defense and branched out to work for local community centers that catered to inner city youth who were unable to afford formal training. I have also competed in various local and national tournaments throughout the north east coast.

In the 90's I appeared in the movie "The Last Dragon" a martial arts film, which was one of the first that gave young black martial artists an opportunity to show their skills. In 1995 I founded and organized the "Salute to the Black Warriors of the Martial Arts". This is a tribute designed to pay homage to the past and present martial artists and pioneers who have helped shape the martial arts in the U.S. today. The yearly event began in New York City and moved to Boston and has been active for several years during Black History month.

My commitment to the arts is preserve and maintain a sense of tradition while still incorporating a modified use of modern techniques.

ACKNOWLEDGEMENTS

My deepest appreciation to two very special women in my life that help to make me the man that I have become, Ms. Doris Thomas and Ms. Willie Ann Smith lovingly, my Mom and Auntie. I thank you both for your love and guidance.

*My dear friend, Malcolm Livingston, training partner, brother of the Arts and co writer of "**I am a Warrior" Virtues,** I thank you for you inspiration and support in making the dream live on. To my student Metaphysics, keep reaching for the stars and always walk in peace. You too have helped me with our **Virtues "I Shall" Always** keep it live in body, mind and action. Thank you for keeping the faith and unconditional respect.*

Master Dwayne Thomas

Virtues

"I Shall Law"

- I shall never use my art in any harmful way except to defend myself when necessary.

I shall never cause trouble.
I shall only walk in peace.
I shall always practice patience.
May I always continue to walk with the King.

"I am a Warrior"

- I am a warrior destined to be king; a master of the self.
True power manifests itself within the soul discarding all in purities and cultivating the inner being.
With strength I shall endure. With love I shall obtain inner peace.
Combined I shall achieve my ultimate goal.
I am a warrior destined to be King; a master of the self.

THE D.A.T. RANKING SYSTEM

The Defensive Arts Training (DAT) ranking system, formally known as Defensive Fitness Training (DFT), has based its principles loosely around the traditional Hard Japanese systems. DAT focuses on building character along with the development and appreciation for the arts. DAT is a contemporary and innovative art form incorporating both the western and eastern principles and practices. It has modified the ranking system for ease of understanding.

In the Traditional Japanese ranking system the words "kyu" meaning boy and "dan" meaning man were used to signify growth and advancement in the arts. Descending progression is also another method used by the Japanese system with an eight "kyu" signifying a lower level than a first "kyu." DAT has modified the use of these terms considering that more women and children have become active in the arts today. Using the ascending levels method allows novices, students, parents, and spectators to understand and recognize advancement more clearly.

The DAT ranking system is comprised of six stages or levels that go from low to high with one signifying the beginning or first stage. The six stages are symbolized by the use of color belts to show growth and advancement within the organization. Some of the basic colors may vary from one style of art to another. White, yellow, green, purple, brown, and black are some of the more traditional colors used by the Japanese schools of the past. DAT has adopted and uses part of this method today with the white belt signifying level one.

There are four different types of promotions within the DAT ranking system. The first is the *Warrior Promotion* where students are required to perform all physical and mental tasks. This is most commonly used, (standard). The second is the *Executive Promotion* which utilizes more intellectual knowledge and oral skills, this is rare. The third is a *Cross-over Promotion*, which is where the student may have had previous training in another discipline or art form and has obtained a rank level he/she wishes to maintain. The fourth is the *Honorary Promotion,* which is rare and requires knowledge of the system and involvement in the arts to a significant capacity. Honorary Promotion should not be used or awarded easily, this is special acknowledgement.

Devotion and enjoyment should be the ultimate goal of the student for training in the arts. Remember that it is not the color of the belt that makes the student but the person wearing it.

D.A.T. Question and Answer list need to know for advancement.

Q-1:   What are the four Rules of Respect in D.A.T.?
1.   Respect yourself.
2.   Respect each other (classmates).
3.   Respect the building.
4.   Respect your parents and elders.

Q-2:   What is a courtesy?
It is a greeting or a salute, a form of bowing.

Q-3:   What is Discipline?
Control.

Q-4:   What is self-discipline?
Self-control.

Q-5:   What is Karate?
Karate is the art of empty hand combat.

Q-6:   What is a Karate KA?
It is one who studies karate seriously.

Q-7:   Why do we practice?
We practice for the perfection of the body, mind, and soul.

Q-8:   When do we practice?
Always.

Q-9:   When do you give up?
Never.

Q-10: What does "I can't" mean?
"I can't" means I am afraid to extend myself.

Q-11: What does "I can" mean?
"I can" means I will because I have the courage.

Q-12: What is courage?
It is the ability to act in spite of fear.

Q-13: What is this thing called the "muck and the mire?"
       The "muck and the mire" is anything necessary to make one a better
       warrior.

Q-14: Speak of failure.
       Failure shall not over take me because my determination to succeed is
       strong enough.

Japanese Translations for Basic Stances 1 to 7

Forward Stance. . . . . Zen-Kut-Su Da-chi
Horse Stance . . . . Kiba-Da-chi
Back Stance . . . . Ko-Kut-su Da-chi
Cat Stance . . . . Neko-ashi Da-chi
Pigeon toe. . . . . San-chin Da-chi
(Pigeon toe stance is also referred to as Hour glass stance.)

Closed legs . . . . Mu-su-bi Da-chi
Open legs . . . . Hei-ko Da-chi

Japanese Basic Counting/Numbers 1 to 10

1—One. . . . . Ichi
2—Two. . . . . Ni
3—Three . . . . San
4—Four . . . . Shi
5—Five. . . . . Go
6—Six. . . . . Roku
7—Seven . . . . Shichi
8—Eight. . . . . Hachi
9—Nine . . . . Ku
10—Ten . . . . Ju

(D.A.T.) Requirements for yellow belt and advanced rank level 2

1. Basic Blocks:
   - 3-point blocking drill
     High, middle, low—single arm
   - 6-point blocking drill
     High, middle, low—alternating arms

2. Basic strikes:
   - Lunge punch
   - Reverse punch
   - Hammer fist
   - Back fist
   - Palm heel
   - Elbow (empi) strike

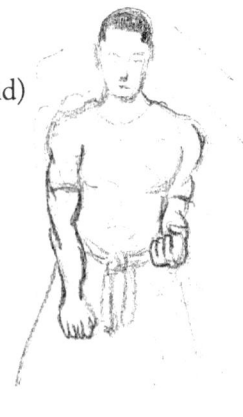

3. Basic Kicks:
   - Front (snap and thrust)
   - Side (balance & thrust)
   - Round house (balance & thrust)

4. Basic stances:
   - Open legs
   - Closed legs
   - Front or forward

5. Katas/forms:
   - Basic form #1—low block front stance
   - Basic form #2—high block front stance knife and strike
   - Basic form #3—Chon-Ji/T Kata
   - Basic form #4—Empi Go (bonus kata not required for yellow belt)

6. Combat combinations:
   a) Punch—punch—kick (front or side)
   b) Kick—punch—punch—kick (front and round)

7. Basic self-defense techniques: 1-5
   1—high block—reverse punch—low block horse stance
   2—high block—palm heel—low block horse stance
   3a—high block—hammer fist—low block horse stance
   3b—high block—shuto/chop low block horse stance
   4—high block—empi/elbow strike

8. Escape techniques:
   1—one arm grab—step back lift and pull away
   2—hand shake or squeeze—grab thumb with finger/knuckles

9. Side stepping Evasion Drill One (1-10 no punishment)

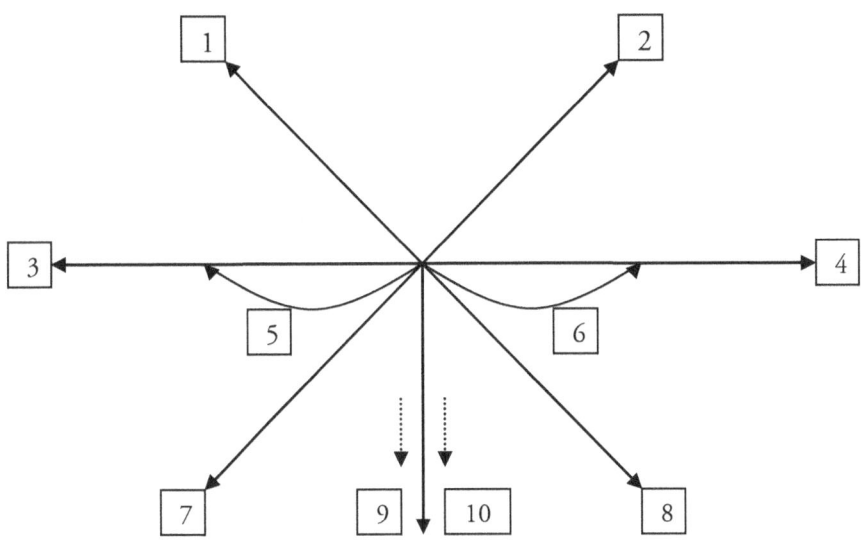

Stage Two:

Self Awareness: Develops balance, coordination, self-control, and discipline.

(D.A.T.) Requirements for green belt and advanced rank level 3

1. Basic & advanced blocks: (Hard and Soft)
   - 3-point blocking drill (single and alternate arm)
   - 6-point blocking drill (single and alternate arm)
   - 8-point blocking drill
   - Circular Fan blocks; inside and outside (open hand).

2. All basic & advanced strikes;
   - Upper cut
   - Hook punch
   - Ridge hand
   - Knife hand
   - Finger strike (one & two) eyes

3. Sweeps:
   - Front sweep
   - Back sweep
   - Dragon sweep

4. Kicks—basic and advanced which include:
   - Hopping Front and Side kicks
   - Hook kicks
   - Crescent kicks (inside and outside)

5. All basic and advanced stances which include:
   - Back stance
   - Cat stance
   - Pigeon toe stance

6. Forms/Katas—All basic forms plus:
   - Hean Shodan (Peaceful mind) one
   - Twin Mountains
   - Geiki Sai Ichi (one)-(attack& smash)
   - Empi (Iron elbow)
   - Sai-Fa (destroy/defeat)*
   - New Birth *

* Note the last two forms on this list are bonus forms and are required at the next level.

7. Combat Combinations;
   1—Punch, punch, kicks (front, side, or round house)
   2—Front kick, punch, punch, hook kick
   3—Express (continuous movement / free flow)

8. Basic Self Defense Techniques and advanced including
   - Wrist, arm locks, and mug or choke holds and throws

9. Some basic knowledge of the history of the arts/D.A.T.
   - Basic History refers to knowing the Founders and the different style which make up (D.A.T), and two or more black belts.

10. Weapons from Bo/staff
    1—First strike
    2—Second strike
    3—New winds

11. Breaking: Two boards punch or kick
12. Exercises:
    - Jumping jacks 100
    - Push-ups 50
    - Sit-ups 50
    - Running 3 to 5 minutes

* Note: The Forms listed for weapons are school forms and are bonus or extra points for candidates going for promotion.

STAGE THREE:

growth and commitment

(D.A.T.) Requirements for purple belt rank level 4

1. All basic blocking drills plus advanced soft blocks;
   - Open hand 6-point blocking drill (Chicken wrist) block
   - Open hand circular outside middle block and outside circular low block.
   - Open hand 10 point blocking drill.

2. All basic strikes plus:
   - Spinning back fist
   - Spinning ridge hand
   - Knuckle punch

3. All basic and advanced kicks plus:
   - Spinning back kick
   - Spinning hook kick
   - Spinning Crescent kick
   - Tornado kick

4. Sweeps/Leg take downs;
   - Front sweep hooking inside and outside leg
   - Front—Iron Broom, drop low and spin
   - Dragon Tail sweep/spinning back sweep
   - Scissors take down

5. Throws and falls (grappling):
   - Hip throw
   - Face fall
   - Back fall—Slap out
   - Front throw back rolls

6. Rolls:
   - Forward roll
   - Shoulder roll
   - Back roll

7. Forms/Katas (Hard and Soft):
    1. Spring leg one (soft form)*
    2. Spring leg two (soft from)*
    3. Spring leg four (soft from)*
    4. New Birth (school) form
    5. Seienchin (attack, conquer & suppress) tradition
    6. Bassai Dai (To storm the Castle)
    7. Empi Ho Hung (open) from created by the late Master Billy Tee Taylor

* Bonus soft forms from the Kung Fu

8. All basic empty-hand techniques plus (1, 2, & 3 knife disarming):
    • Frontal mug 1: knife to stomach, push, grab, side step, turn horse stands, elbow back or shock.
    • Frontal mug 2: knife to throat, grab wrist with both hands turn & take down
    • Frontal mug 3: lunge to stomach, X block low, trap twist lock, break or control take down

* Note: Katas/forms may vary but students are required to know at least two of the seven. At this time it is very important to take your time to develop and perfect understanding and technique. If it takes you more time on one kata then use the time to do it well and do not worry about doing many or all.

STAGE FOUR:

---

strength and knowledge of technique, confidence, & awareness

(D.A.T.) Requirements for brown belt and advanced rank level 5

1. All basic and advanced blocking drills.

2. All basic and advanced strikes, kicks, and punches.
   - Jump kicks/hopping
   - Jumping side kick
   - Jumping front kick
   - Jumping round house
   - Jumping hook kick
   - Jumping spinning hook kick
   - Jumping spinning back kick

3. All basic and advanced sweeps.

4. All basic throws and rolls.

5. Katas/Forms—All basic forms plus:
   - Maroshi (To penetrate the fortress) classic school form *open
   - Bassai Dai (To Strom the / Castle) Traditional Japanese
   - Kanku Dai (To look to the Sky) Traditional Japanese
   - Jion (Staint) Traditional Japanese
   - Black Dragon *pen
   - Kamikaze (Divine Thunder/the way of the suicide warrior) school form *open

*   considered nontraditional classic forms

6. All basic and advanced self defense techniques empty hand plus:
   - 3 or 4 knife disarming
   - three frontal attacks one rear

7. Breaks: Two or three boards, two different strikes:
   - punches
   - kicks
   - elbows
   - chops
   - head

All students are required to write a one page report on what it takes to be a black belt and why they wish to be become one.

All candidates for brown belt rank should do community service to learn the value of giving back and humility.

Exercise Requirement:

All Basic Calisthenics including stretching and breathing exercises—B series, 1 to 8:

1. One arm raise
2. Two hand push the ski
3. Forward stretch (reach toes)
4. Side stretch (reach left & right)
5. Lifting arms
6. Bow & arrow shoot the eagle
7. Neck rolls
8. Merry go round

Endurance drills:

- 1 to 2 miles run.
- 100 kicks
- 200 Punches
- 200 Blocks

*   Note: because it can take many years to prefect a kata/form please do not rush to know all the forms within the system, but find the one or two that you like that fits you and try to own it by doing it well.

STAGE FIVE:

self-confidence, sharp technique, and endurance.

(D.A.T.) Requirement For Black Belt Rank Level 6

BLACK BELT candidates must be in top Physical and Mental Health at time of testing.

1. All basic and advanced, Strikes, Blocks, Kicks, Sweeps and Stances are to be performed physical and verbally.

2. One Weapon of choice: bo/ staff, sai, knives, sticks, or kama sickles.

Four breaking techniques:*

1. Reverse Punch
2. Hammer First
3. Elbow strike
4. Side kick or Front kick

All Self Defense Techniques plus weapons disarming.

*   Optional—One personal creation

All basic translation of basic numbers, (1 to 10) in Japanese.

All basic translation of stances, (1 to 7) in Japanese.

All candidates should have participated in competition before testing and lead class in calisthenics and basic drill.

Knowledge of basic human anatomy:

*   Skeletal
*   Muscular system

Cardiovascular

Advanced Katas/ Forms (1 to 6):

1. Seienchin (attack, conquer & suppress) traditional Japanese Goju
2. Bassai Dai (To storm the Castle)*(bonus) traditional Shotokan
3. Empi Ho Hung (open) from created by the late Master Billy Tee Taylor
4. Kanku Dai (To look to the Sky) Traditional Shotokan
5. Jion (Staint) Traditional Shotokan
6. Black Dragon-open (Chinese Goju)

STAGE SIX:

Self-awareness, self-confidence, humility, appreciation & devotion.

Defensive Arts Training Promotions

Test Sheet

Student's Name: _____ Age: _____ Date: _____

Rank: _____ Pass: Yes ☐ No ☐ Advance to: _____

Intellectual Knowledge	Proficient	Satisfactory	Not Satisfactory	Comments
Q&A				
Virtue				
I Shall Law				
History				

Physical Conditioning	Proficient	Satisfactory	Not Satisfactory	Comments
Jumping Jacks				
Push-ups				
Sit-ups				
Stretching				

Techniques & Skills	P	S	NS	Comments	Techniques & Skills	P	S	NS	Comments
3-point drill					Front kick				
6-point drill					Side kick				
8-point drill					Round kick				
10-point drill					Hook kick				
Stances					Crescent				
Open legs					Strikes				
Close legs					Lunge				
Horse					Reverse				
Forward					Back fist				
Back					Hammer				
Cat					Elbow				
Pigeon Toe					Palm strike				

Final Notes:_____

_____

Bonus and Advanced Points

Signature: _____
Date: _____

Defensive Arts Training Promotions

Test Sheet

Katas /Forms	(10 to 8) Proficient	(7 to 6) Satisfactory	(5 to 3) Not Satisfactory	Comments
Balance				
Stance				
Pattern				
Execution				

Kumite / Sparring	(10 to 8) Proficient	(7 to 6) Satisfactory	(5 to 3) Not Satisfactory	Comments
Technique				
Endurance				
Execution				
Heart / Courage				

Breaking	(10 to 8) Proficient	(7 to 6) Satisfactory	(5 to 3) Not Satisfactory	Comments
Technique				
Level of difficulty				
Number of boards				
Execution				

Scoring Range: 10 =High, 7 = Middle, & 5= low (needs more practice)

Final score: _____

_____

Personal notes: _____

www.ingramcontent.com/pod-product-compliance
Lightning Source LLC
Chambersburg PA
CBHW061229280526
45784CB00006B/2688